D0506938

HOW TO COOK
THE PERFECT DAY

Nikki McClure

SASQUATCH BOOKS
SEATTLE

Printed in Canada
Published by Sasquatch Books
Distributed by PGW/Perseus
15 14 13 12 11 10   9 8 7 6 5 4 3 2 1

Cover design and art: Nikki McClure
Interior design and composition: Sarah Plein
Interior art: Nikki McClure

Library of Congress Cataloging-in-Publication Data is available.

ISBN-13: 978-1-57061-686-0
ISBN-10: 1-57061-686-8

Sasquatch Books
119 South Main Street, Suite 400
Seattle, WA 98104
(206) 467-4300
www.sasquatchbooks.com
custserv@sasquatchbooks.com

Mixed Sources
Product group from well-managed forests,
controlled sources and recycled wood or fiber
www.fsc.org Cert no. SW-COC-000952
© 1996 Forest Stewardship Council
FSC

Passion(ate) consum(ate) inti(ate)

"The secret to cooking is 99 percent love," said a French chef who created the most perfect chocolate cake that I will ever eat. You can follow recipes exactly, leveling off the cup of flour with a knife, but food must be created with love if it is to be eaten with passion. Food nourishes and electrifies the heart, and it is this spirit that makes us most alive. I have collected perfect food moments where my heart sang out with each bite—morning, noon, and night. May your heart sing as you cook the perfect day.

Good Morning Forage

I walk barefoot in Southern California after a rainstorm and tiptoe over downed limbs, breathing fresh pine air. Plans of the day begin to form and lists are half scribbled in my brain, made sharper and clearer by the chill. I eat a few bites of an apple still cold from the night, blown down from a tree. Figs hang low, heavy with ripeness, and birds call out over pomegranates split open. Eating each seed one by one, admiring the crystal gems, I am unable to turn back once the deed is done and I have plundered this ruby mine.

Apple
Fig
Pomegranate
And anything else you can find

Collect and eat.

Anacortes Peaches and Waffles

There is a bowl full of roundness and peaches ripe. Island seawater breeze brightens thoughts and waffle irons press out warmth. Peaches are cut over the waffles and the juice drips down ridges and fills valleys, forming an archipelago. This is how a baby family feeds a multitude of friends.

> 1¾ cups flour (use a combination of whole wheat and unbleached all-purpose flours or even quinoa and corn flours are nice—find your perfect ratio)
> 2 teaspoons baking powder
> ½ teaspoon salt
> 1 tablespoon sugar
> 3 eggs, separated
> 1½ cups milk
> 4 tablespoons melted butter or oil, plus more as needed
> Fresh peaches
> Maple syrup

Sift together flours, baking powder, salt, and sugar. Beat egg yolks. Stir in milk and melted butter. Pour wet ingredients into flour mixture. Beat with a few swift strokes, but not too much. Beat egg whites until stiff and fold into batter.

Pour batter over heated waffle iron brushed with a bit of melted butter or oil. Cover. When steaming stops, the waffle is done. Cut peaches over waffles and drizzle with *real* maple syrup, please.

Poppy Seed Rolls

Determining who will be your companion (the one with whom bread is shared) begins with how bread is prepared. You knead the dough until it gives in just a bit and then slowly moves back on its own accord. You must persuade the gluten to stretch and sigh. Then you must wait and wait for the resting dough to rise and grow, then start over and wait some more. The longer you wait, the better the bread will be. Once it is baked, it is impossible to let the bread be. Steam escapes from your mouth as you inhale more than you can eat of the hot bread. It is the essence of heart and home that is consumed. To yield to this kneading is to give in to love.

2 tablespoons active dry yeast
1½ cups lukewarm water
A drop of honey
3 cups whole wheat flour, divided

3 cups unbleached all-purpose flour, divided
¼ cup melted butter
¼ cup honey or molasses
2 teaspoons salt
2 tablespoons poppy seeds

Sprinkle yeast into water. Add a drop of honey and let stand 5 minutes. Mix in 1 cup of each of the flours. Cover with a clean towel and let rise for at least 1 hour.

Beat together melted butter, ¼ cup honey, salt, and poppy seeds. Add to yeast mixture.

Knead in the remaining 2 cups each of the flours, adding ½ cup at a time. Knead for 15 minutes, or until the dough feels soft like your earlobe. Roll dough in an oiled bowl and cover. Let it rise in a cozy place for a few hours or more, until it has doubled in size. Tear off pieces and form into turtles, alligators, snails, and other favorite creatures, and arrange on a baking sheet. Let dough rise one more time.

Bake in preheated oven at 425°F for 15 to 20 minutes. Let rolls cool if you can stand to wait.

Picnic Rendezvous

The most perfect strawberries are eaten at a hidden rendezvous. The basket is emptied of mysterious surprises. Lovingly formed turtles, alligators, and snails of poppy seed bread were baked full of secrets: our smiles are now shared by the world.

Poppy seed rolls
Garlic, sliced into thin slivers
Avocados, sliced
Watercress
Mustard

Put together sandwiches using all ingredients. I recommend eating dark chocolate afterward.

Lime Ginger Ale

2-inch piece ginger, peeled
4 cups water
1 teaspoon peppercorns
1 cup sugar or honey (or more if desired)
Juice from 12 limes
4 cups soda water

Grind ginger to a paste. Mix with water and peppercorns. Bring mixture to a boil and then reduce to simmer for 5 minutes. Strain through cheesecloth. Mix in sugar and lime juice, then chill. Add soda water just before serving.

Green Bean Supreme

Green Bean Girl is me at six years old picking beans fresh from the vine and then snapping them into my mouth. I trip over a vine and impale my knee on a garden stake. A long ride to the hospital, some stitches, and three lollipops later, I am back in the garden eating more beans.

Fresh is the best. But if you must cook the beans, then barely cover the bottom of a skillet with water. Lay the beans in the skillet and heat. Cover and steam just until the beans turn a vivid green. And if you really must be fancy, try the following salad.

1 tablespoon olive oil
1½-inch piece ginger, peeled and grated
2 tablespoons fresh orange juice
1 teaspoon poppy seeds
Salt and pepper
2 carrots, peeled and cut julienne
1 small fennel bulb, very thinly sliced
¼ pound green beans, cut into long strips

Whisk together oil, ginger, orange juice, poppy seeds, salt, and pepper. Toss carrots, fennel, and green beans with dressing just before serving.

Moroccan Mint Tea

I was in Paris with Stella. We ventured into the North African part of the city just as the riot police vans were unloading. Body-shielded police lined up, making a wall of drawn loaded tear gas guns with canisters to spare. Protestors came around the corner with bright signs and foreign chants demanding release of prisoners and immigration rights. We slipped along the edge of the sidewalk into the relative calm of a corner market. I asked for tea and was handed a small, ornately painted golden glass that my hand fit around. I was warmed immediately. The minted steam opened my mind and soothed my worries. One sip of sweetness and I knew I wanted more.

> **1 tablespoon gunpowder tea**
> **Big handful of fresh spearmint (or 2 tablespoons dried)**
> **¼ cup honey**
> **Boiling water**
> **A few drops of orange flower water**

Rinse out your teapot with some boiling water. Add tea, mint, honey, and boiling hot water. Let steep for 3 minutes. Add orange flower water. Serve in small glasses and sweeten, if desired. Sip for hours, enjoying a least three glassfuls.

Lovely Gingerbread Cake

It's a high tea time-out to assess the day that is almost done. Work is finished. Now it is the beginning of family/self/love time when you can do whatever you want, but first you need some energy to continue.

¼ cup olive oil or butter
½ cup molasses
½ cup maple syrup
⅔ cup boiling water
1 teaspoon baking soda
1 egg, beaten
¼ cup prunes, dates, or any
   dried fruit, finely chopped
⅓ cup applesauce

1 tablespoon freshly grated
   ginger
1½ cup quinoa flour (wheat is
   fine too)
1 teaspoon cinnamon
1 teaspoon ginger powder
¼ teaspoon ground cloves
Powdered sugar

Preheat the oven to 350°F. Butter a 9-inch-square pan.

Combine oil, molasses, syrup, and water in a large bowl. Stir in baking soda, egg, prunes, applesauce, and grated ginger.

Sift flour with cinnamon, ginger powder, and ground cloves. Stir into batter. Pour batter into prepared pan and bake for 35 minutes, or until a toothpick inserted into the cake comes out clean.

Make a paper-cut stencil. Place on top of cake and dust with powdered sugar. Remove stencil. Eat cake warm.

Nettle Soup

Nettle soup is a spring tonic and a restorative, spirit-infused strength inducer. Honest. It heals all the wounds of winter and prepares the body for the wakening season.

Harvest nettles with scissors when they are young and tender. (This is the best part! Absorb the vibrant green of early spring in the woods and listen to birds singing.) Wear rubber gloves even while washing and trimming the nettles. Once wilted, a nettle loses its sting.

Make soup stock with a week's worth of potato, apple, ginger, and carrot peels and trimmings; mushroom, spinach, and parsley stems; onion skins, seaweed, and old leeks. Boil in 2 quarts water and reduce to a rich brown stock. Strain well, reserving the liquid and sending the rest to the compost.

> 1 tablespoon olive oil
> ½ onion, diced
> 2 yellow potatoes, diced, or 2 cups cooked rice
> Salt and pepper
> 4 cups homemade soup stock (see above), vegetable stock, or
>   chicken stock
> 1 bag nettle shoots, stems removed

In a soup pot, heat oil over medium heat. Sauté onion until translucent. Add potatoes or rice and stir for 1 minute, then season with salt and pepper. Pour in stock and simmer until the potatoes are tender. Add nettle leaves and simmer for 15 minutes. You can blend some or all or none of the soup, depending on how you like it.

Serve and eat it all up, drinking down the last drops to nourish your soul.

P is for Potluck and Perfect Day Curry

In her essay "W is for Wanton," M.F.K. Fisher gives her gourmand advice on the time-honored way to woo a mate through the perfect dinner. She prescribes a simple salad and consommé, followed by a rich curry and rice, then a light desert of fruit. Once this seemed the perfect end to a perfect day, but now I am much more concerned about caring for a community. The most perfect dinner of this perfect day would be one where your neighbors, family, and friends come together to share food and a collective future.

3 cups fish or vegetable stock
1 lemongrass stalk
1 tablespoon olive oil
1 onion, diced
1 carrot, chopped
1 block of tofu, cubed
1 potato, diced
1 bunch of kale, cut chiffonade
1 can coconut milk

½ cup fresh pineapple
2 tomatoes, chopped
Thai basil or cilantro, chopped
Thai red curry paste (start with ½ teaspoon, then add more to taste—remember, there will be children present!)
Juice from 1 lime

Bring stock to a boil in a medium pot. Pound lemongrass stalk and add to stock. Simmer for 15 minutes.

Heat wok or large sauté pan. Add oil, onion, and carrot. Stir for a few minutes. Add tofu, potato, kale, and half of the coconut milk. Stir in hot stock and simmer for 10 minutes, or until potatoes are tender. Add pineapple, tomatoes, and some basil. In a medium bowl, mix curry paste with ½ cup cooking liquid, stir in remaining coconut milk, and then pour all back into pan. Top with basil and add lime juice just before serving. Pour over rice, serving others before you.

Blood Orange Salad

There is always some wooing and wantonness to indulge in, so I save my salad until last. Blood orange salad contrasts the purity and simplicity of lettuce, olive oil, and vinegar with lusty blood. Leaves are torn on the beach with the setting sun, and there is nothing but the gentle rolling of the waves to focus on.

1 head romaine lettuce
2 blood oranges
12 oil-cured olives
3 tablespoons olive oil
1 tablespoon rice vinegar
Pinch of salt

Wash and dry lettuce. Tear leaves into pieces and put in a large salad bowl.

Cut oranges into slices and remove peel with knife. Put sections in bowl.

Remove pits from olives and coarsely chop. Add to oil and vinegar in a small bowl. Salt to taste. Mix well. Add dressing to salad, tossing lettuce and oranges to coat. Serve on the beach.

Celestial Apple Pie

There is a lunar eclipse signaling the beginning of spring. I wish on a comet night after night. Celestial apple pie steam is sent into orbit signaling an end to a perfect day and welcoming another. It turns my home into a lighthouse of coddled warmth.

6 apples	¼ cup pecans or hazelnuts
2 pears	(optional)
Freshly grated nutmeg	2 cups unbleached all-purpose
1 teaspoon cinnamon	flour
¼ cup sweetener (anything but	¾ cup cold butter
white sugar!)	10 tablespoons very cold ice
1 tablespoon cornstarch	water

Preheat the oven to 400°F.

Peel, core, and slice apples and pears. Toss with nutmeg, cinnamon, sweetener, and cornstarch. Set aside.

Toast nuts in a skillet, let cool, then chop very fine.

Sift flour. Cut butter into flour with two knives like my Grandma or use a pastry cutter. Sprinkle water onto flour 1 tablespoon at a time. Mix until a ball of pastry dough forms. Divide in half and roll out one half on lightly floured board. Gently place rolled dough in pie pan and top with fruit mixture. Roll out second half of dough and place on top of the pie. Seal edges and cut slits in the top for steam to escape to the heavens.

Bake for 15 minutes at 400°F, then reduce temperature to 350°F and continue baking 35 to 40 minutes, or until pie crust is golden brown. Cool on the porch but not on the sill of a second story window.

Midnight Morning Biscuits

The day is almost over, and there is one last chance to warm the hearth and share some treats with friends. I have reached an efficient biscuit-making time of fifteen minutes from start to finish, and the kitchen is even clean, too. Eat a few at midnight, then save some for the morning to drizzle with honey. Remember all that happened the day before and dream up the day ahead.

2 cups any flour
Big pinch of salt
3 teaspoons baking powder
4 tablespoons butter
¾ to 1 cup milk

Preheat the oven to 450°F.

Mix together flour, salt, and baking powder in a large bowl. Mix butter into flour mixture by rubbing and crumbling it with your fingers until you have pea-sized crumbs. Stir in milk. Add sesame, poppy, anise, or fennel seeds to make "Fancy Biscuits." Knead ever so lightly and then gently pat dough flat. Cut into circles, place on baking sheet, and let sit for 15 minutes.

Bake for 12 minutes, or until biscuits are golden. Clean up any mess while biscuits are baking. Eat at least one biscuit immediately.

Eat with friends. Eat outside.

How to Cook the Perfect Day was originally self-published in 1997. It was one of my first projects where I experimented with making paper-cut images. The pictures are paper cut with an X-Acto knife. I have been making paper cuttings ever since.

The cookbook was a small photocopied booklet with pages folded and bound with rings to facilitate adding additional food moments and recipes of memory. My original copy is now crusted with gingerbread batter and stained by buttery fingers. In this new edition some recipes have been changed a little as I have experimented with new tastes, but nothing has been changed too much. The memories are still there. This day is still perfect.

If I could make another perfect day I would have to now add Jay T.'s blueberry pancakes that he cooks every morning, Lois's lemon cake that disappears at every picnic, any of Finn's inspired soups, a salty massaged kale salad, a bellyful of berries, and a mug of chicken broth. Oh, plus a fried egg salad! There are always more recipes to discover and many more perfect days ahead.

Make your own!

Thank you to all the cooks who made
this perfect day possible.
Don't forget 99 percent love.